OVER MY SHOULDER

(Lenten Thoughts for Imperfect Christians)

DAVID
DUNN-WILSON

For Richard and Carole

Amicus verus est rara avis

**An 'UNAUTHORISED FOREWORD'
presented in response to the above dedication!**

Revd. Professor David Dunn-Wilson is a learned man, who carries his learning lightly. He has a smile on his face emanating from a 'warmed heart' and a winsome wit which helps build relationships with colleagues, staff, students and strangers alike.

Those who have known him in the past, throughout his long and varied ministry and those who continue to know him as a pastor and friend today have been truly blessed.

In recent years I have come to know David well as a minister, lecturer, encourager and friend. This word from me will embarrass David but he puts many of us to shame by his Wesley-like disciplined dedication to early morning devotions and to continuing study. The fruit of his devotional life is shared in these Lenten reflections based on the Book of Proverbs in the Bible.

Having spent time with David's thoughts whilst editing the text, I want to commend this sharing as a Lenten discipline and devotion. It will not disappoint you, nor will God, found in and through Jesus Christ, who continues to speak through his saints by the Holy Spirit.

Revd Richard Jackson: Coordinator of Cliff College International Training Centre (CCITC) & Carole.

A CONFESSION AND AN INVITATION

Each year, like many Christians, I look for a book to be part of my Lenten devotions and there is never any shortage of excellent candidates. However, this year, I had a problem. It wasn't their fault – it was mine. I once read of an old Methodist preacher who described himself by saying, "I am just a jobbing Christian – one who has been long at his trade but not yet master of it" – and reluctantly I had to admit that that was me too – 'just a jobbing Christian'. Compared with me, all those Lenten writers seemed so competent, expert and assured. They were like cordon bleu chefs whose recipes I might admire but could never hope to cook.

So, what was I to do? Why not write my own Lenten meditations for each day as I went along? But where should I look for inspiration?

I found myself re-reading in the Bible, The Book of Proverbs, which I have always liked for its wit and wisdom and I was impressed afresh by how practical it is. I decided that it would make great Lenten reading, especially if I selected a verse each day, listened to its message and then wrote a little about it as an aide memoire.

Gradually, I gathered together the Wise Men's lessons and the harvest became this book – a book by 'a jobbing Christian'. It was then that I wondered, "Are there other 'jobbing Christians' out there?

Are there other believers who, like me, love to be in 'The Way' but often wander from it? Would they like to travel with me through Lent?"

So, if it that is you, please come and join me. As I think aloud on paper, lean over my shoulder and feel free to take anything that is useful. Use my reflections to trigger your own deeper insights - and just leave the rest.

Let God speak to you through The Wise Men as he continues to speak to me.

David Dunn-Wilson

Eastbourne

December 2015

N.B. (For quotations, I have used the Contemporary English Version of the Bible because it seems to me to capture the mood of Proverbs so vividly but, by all means, compare it with other versions and to gain additional insights. I have chosen Key Verses for each day, but there is also plenty of 'food for thought' in the remainder of the passages chosen for reading.)

JUST IN CASE....

Just in case The Book of Proverbs is not one of your favourite 'Sunday afternoon walks' in the Bible and seems like strange territory, may I introduce you to the Wise Men? It seems that, in the ancient world, the idea of 'wisdom' was very important. 'Wisdom' was a very practical word which meant skill in making the right decisions and then doing the right thing. Of course, the Jews knew that only God is perfectly 'wise' but they also believed that God shared the gift of 'wisdom' with certain, chosen, people who could then guide others in practical, godly living

Among these chosen people were, the writers of Proverbs and the book is a collection of their wise sayings. The most important contributor is said to be the great King Solomon (especially famous for his wisdom) but there are also sayings from Agur, Lemuel and many anonymous Wise Men. Amazingly, they seem to have a word of wise guidance for almost every aspect of life.

I have selected just a few of the 'wise sayings' - the ones through which God has spoken to me afresh by his Wise Men. The first Christians certainly admired and quoted Proverbs but they always read it in the light of an even greater revelation of God's wisdom. Like them, I encounter God's Wisdom in the person of, "Jesus Christ crucified.... the power and the wisdom of God" (I Corinthians 1:24).

Jesus will be my guide too.

So let's begin.

TABLE OF CONTENTS

1. THE DARK SIDE OF THE GOSPEL 11
   Proverbs 1:20-33 11
2. DIVINE COMMON SENSE 13
   Proverbs 2:1-9 13
3. LIFE'S INDIAN QUEENS 15
   Proverbs 3:1-10 15
4. ROOTS AND FRUITS 17
   Proverbs 3:13-18 17
5. 'THOU SHALT NOT SLUG!' 19
   Proverbs 6:6-11 19
6. BETTER THE DEVIL YOU KNOW 21
   Proverbs 6:12-19 21
7. PLAYING WITH FIRE 23
   Proverbs 6:20-29 23
8. THE BUNDLE OF LIFE 25
   Proverbs 8:32-36 25
9. PILLARS 27
   Proverbs 9:1-9 27
10. MORE PILLARS 29
    Proverbs 9:1-9 29
11. THE ULTIMATE REVERENCE 31
    Proverbs 9:10-18 31
12. SILENCE IS GOLDEN 33
    Proverbs 10:1-14 33

13. A BLESSING TO MYSELF 35

    Proverbs 11: 15-23 35

14. MONEY! MONEY! MONEY! 37

    Proverbs 11:24-28 37

15. R.S.P.C.A. 39

    Proverbs 12:5-10 39

16. MY WORD IS MY BOND 41

    Proverbs 12:16-22 41

17. GRIST TO THE MILL 43

    Proverbs 12:23-28 43

18. STAY FOCUSSED 45

    Proverbs 13:14-22 45

19. ON WITH THE MOTLEY! 47

    Proverbs 14:6-14 47

20. RELAXED CHRISTIANS 49

    Proverbs 14:29-35 49

21. BEING GRUNTLED 51

    Proverbs 15:1-10 51

22. PLANNING AND TRUSTING 53

    Proverbs 16:1-9 53

23. CONTEMPT ON ALL MY PRIDE 55

    Proverbs 16:10-23 55

24. CLOSING THE FLOOD-GATES 57

    Proverbs 17:7-16 57

25. REDEEMING GOSSIP 59

    Proverbs 18:1-8 59

26. TIMID FAITH 61

Proverbs 18:10-19 61

27. PASSING THE BUCK 63

Proverbs 19:1-12 63

28. "....A LENDER BE" 65

Proverbs 19:13-20 65

29. THE GLORIOUS LIBERTY 67

Proverbs 19:20-29 67

30. GOD'S SEARCHLIGHT 69

Proverbs 20:23-30 69

31. RULES AND REGULATIONS 71

Proverbs 12:1-8 71

32. LORD, I'M TIRED! 73

Proverbs 22:4-16 73

33. CHRISTIAN CONSERVATISM 75

Proverbs 22:17-29 75

34. SHUTTING MY EYES 77

Proverbs 24:1-12 77

35. DANGEROUS LIASONS 79

Proverbs 25:21-28 79

36. FUELLING FELLOWSHIP 81

Proverbs 26:17-28 81

37. SENSITIVITY 83

Proverbs 27:8-14 83

38. 'FOLDING MY LEGS' WITH GOD 85

Proverbs 27:17-27 85

39. IGNORANCE AND BLISS 87

    Proverbs 29:12-22 87

40. THE HIDE AND SEEK GOD 89

    Proverbs 30:1-10 89

P.S. ISN'T IT A PITY? 91

+ ONE DAY 91

1. THE DARK SIDE OF THE GOSPEL

Proverbs 1:20-33

Key verse:-1:31 "Now you will eat the fruit of what you have done"

I don't like Lady Wisdom's idea that, sometimes, God leaves me to, 'eat the fruit of what I have done' but I am afraid that she is right. Persistent sin has a cumulative effect (v.24) and it can warp my judgement so badly that God brings me to my senses by simply letting me have my own way. It isn't until I'm biting into 'bitter fruit' that I realise how stupid I've been.

Perhaps I shouldn't be surprised. Enlightened parents allow their children to learn by their own mistakes so I mustn't think that God is being unfair if he does the same. He is a loving parent who knows that, at times, the only way that he can make me listen to him is by allowing me to make a fool of myself. Now that I stop to think about it, I can recall some very embarrassing occasions when he has proved his point!

It reminds me of those spine-tingling words from *Judges 5:20,* "The stars from their courses fought against Sisera" (*KJV*). The lesson is simple. If I resist God, I will swim against the tide of a moral universe. God has made me for loving, glad obedience and, if I choose another way, things will go wrong. Nations refusing to love each other will eat the 'bitter fruit' of war. Those whose economic greed changes climates will eat the 'bitter fruit' of fire and flood. The unjust will know the bitterness of reprisal and tyrant will eat 'the bitter fruit' of revolution. It may take time but it will happen. That is just the way things are and I myself am no exception to that cosmic law.

Jesus' stark warnings against repeatedly rejecting him (e.g. *Luke* 13:24ff.) remind me that there is a dark side to the Gospel The Good News becomes Bad News for those who refuse to hear it. If I squander God's love by persistent disobedience, I too will find that life will twist and turn in my hands and, eventually, I will eat 'bitter fruit'. I need to know when having my own way is proving disastrous, so that I can change course and move in God's way

TODAY'S RESOLVE

Today, I will be especially on my guard against habitual sins.

"Lord, alert me to danger areas in my life and, if things go wrong, use them to teach me. Amen!"

DAY TWO

2. DIVINE COMMON SENSE

Proverbs 2:1-9

Key verse:-2:6 "All wisdom comes from the Lord, and so do common sense and understanding."

This brings back a memory! "Use your common sense, boy!" It was my Latin master's favourite phrase when he saw me gazing blankly at my book. To me, there seemed to be no connection between Caesar's *Gallic Wars* and 'common sense'. Certainly, it never crossed my mind that common sense had anything to do with God. But here it is, "Common sense comes from the Lord." It is a facet of God-given 'wisdom', a sort of practical 'know how' which understands the way that life *really* works.

I always thought that common sense was a natural part of being human but it seems that *genuine* common sense is something that I need to be given. I'm told in these verses that it is when I 'listen, beg and search' that common sense is given'. I suppose this is because my human common sense is faulty, infected by sin like everything else about me. It needs to be replaced by *God's* common sense – but what is the difference?

Samuel was shown the difference. God tells him, "People judge others by what they look like but I judge people by what is in their hearts". (*I Samuel.*

16:8) That's the difference! God's common sense has X-ray vision. When God makes his judgements, God looks right through the superficial things that I take so seriously – the way people look and dress, the houses they live in, the cars they drive, the way they speak. For God, what really counts are the hidden motives, the true feelings and the genuineness of commitment.

So God's common sense and mine are different. Mine depends on what *I* can do with a situation but his is based upon what *God* can do with it. What is foolish to me is often sensible to God. That's why Jesus taught his disciples to stop depending on their own faulty common sense and see everything through God's eyes, trusting him to meet all their needs.

I think that part of my problem is that I belong to the 'fast food' society which thinks that the human, 'common sense' way is always quickest and easiest. I can see now that that is not God's way. God is immensely patient and takes time to bring plans to fruition. It's high time that I accepted God's offer of divine common sense. I ought to have learned long ago to adopt his perspective and live at God's pace.

TODAY'S RESOLVE

Today, I will really try to look at the world through God's eyes.

"Lord, save me from judging by first impressions and seeking quick results. May I dismiss nothing as impossible until you have confirmed that it is so? Amen!"

DAY THREE

3. LIFE'S INDIAN QUEENS

Proverbs 3:1-10

Key verses:-3:5-6 "With all your heart you must trust the Lord... Always let him lead you...and he will clear the road....."

Long before the era of *satnavs,* I still remember my parents preparing for our holiday in Cornwall- a considerable adventure in those days. The packing was completed, including my precious bucket and spade (although I always hoped for new ones when we finally arrived) and then the map would be carefully studied to find the best route. We would set off very early in the morning and my mother would sit with the map open on her lap, an unerring guide. However, not even she could save us. Every year it was the same. When we reached Indian Queens, our journey would grind to a halt in a seemingly endless traffic-jam. I remember it well because I was fascinated by the place name (later I learned that the name came from the sign of an old coaching in which had an Indian on one side and Queen Victoria on the other – but nobody seems sure)

 I wonder if that's a picture of the Wise Man's meaning here. He is saying that, when I have decisions to make in life, I must not just dash off thinking that I know best. I must 'study the map', take time for God to show me the right way to go. It was while I was thinking about this that I noticed that an older version of this text says, "In all your ways *acknowledge* God". Wondering exactly what 'acknowledging God' might mean I dug deeper and find that the original word is more profound than I had expected. Apparently, it combines three verbs – *observe, care about* and *praise.* Thinking about this, I realise that, if I did those three things before making decisions I would certainly be more likely to allow God to choose my road.

But what about that Indian Queens traffic jam? That's a true picture too. Travelling along God's chosen way will have its problems – its traffic jams. My Lord does not promise me trouble-free travel. I am not alone on the road of life. Quite apart from my own careless driving, there are other bad drivers to make travel dangerous. There are tempting short-cuts to divert me from the proper route. There are accidents and frustrating delays to bring my travelling to a halt. But – and it is a big BUT – The Wise man assures me that, if 'I trust God with my whole heart', he 'will clear the road for me.' I need to remember that he is my constant travelling-companion.

TODAY'S RESOLVE

Today, I will really take time to make sure that I am doing the right thing.

"Lord, give me patience to wait for your guidance and to trust you to bring me safely through life's traffic-jams' Amen!"

DAY FOUR

4. ROOTS AND FRUITS

Proverbs 3:13-18

Key verse:-3:18 "Wisdom is a life-giving tree, the source of happiness for all that hold on to her"

       I've just come back from my early morning walk in the park where I thought about these words as I looked at the trees. Years ago, I saw those trees planted to make a wind-break. Originally, they all looked equally small and vulnerable but now some are sturdy and large while others have almost withered away. I'm no expert on trees but I guess that perhaps the problem lies out of sight below the ground. Perhaps the weaklings' roots have not found enough nourishment.

In some ways, my life is like those trees. Most people begin equally vulnerably and how they develop depends largely upon their early nourishment. It may take time for the effects of malnutrition finally to appear but it *will* happen. That applies to spiritual malnutrition too. There must have been times when I resented being taken to Sunday School and regarded 'church' as a waste of good playing-time. What I didn't realise was that I was being spiritually nourished. Without knowing it, I was absorbing godliness. Christian teaching and values were seeping into my soul to feed and strengthen me for later life.

What would have happened to me if it had been different? What if my parents had said (as many do) "We're not going to force religion down his throat. He can make up his own mind when he is older"? Spiritually, life would never have been a level laying-field and I might never have understood enough about the Christian faith either to accept or reject it. It would have changed my life completely and I would be a totally different person today.

The proverb says that 'wisdom' (that is, God-given understanding) is a 'life-giving tree' because it has its roots in God himself and draws its nourishment straight from him. He invites me to pick its fruit of true happiness but it still worries me that, far too often, people can look at me and see a man whose happiness is hidden – a man who is just as tetchy and impatient as everybody else. Often, I'm not much of an advert for Christian joy! I need to give that some attention!

TODAY'S RESOLVE

Today, I will remember that I may be the only example of 'being a Christian' that the people I meet today will ever see.

"Lord, teach me the art of being truly joyful without always being mindlessly and annoyingly cheerful. Amen!"

DAY FIVE

5. 'THOU SHALT NOT SLUG!'

Proverbs 6:6-11

Key verse:-6:6 "You lazy people can learn from watching an anthill."

I admit that the very mention of ants makes me shudder. I can still remember my encounter with some ferocious African Fire Ants! The Wise Man's Harvester Ants may have been much less fierce but their secret of success was the same – their ability to work hard in community.

It is from the ants that the 'lazy people' are to learn the value of hard work in cooperation with others. I still prefer the punch of *The King James' Version's* sonorous, "Go to the ant thou sluggard!" with its splendid verb 'to slug' – to be lazy. The Sluggard is one of the Wise Man's repertory company of actors. It seems to me that the Sluggard is *Proverbs'* unattractive clown, appearing from time to time; a sadly comical character whose antics reveal uncomfortable truths about his audience.

For me, he uncovers one particular 'sluggardly' aspect of my own spiritual life and Lent is a good time to face up to it. The sluggard procrastinates. When forced to act, he goes on grumbling, offering all sorts of excuses and imagining all sorts of reasons for failure ((6:9f.20:4, 23:13) Sometimes, there's a streak of the Sluggard in me. Despite all my good intentions, I put things off and I am

19

wonderfully adept at excusing myself. Jesus warned me about this kind of spiritual laziness. He told me to deal with today's issues *today* because tomorrow will bring its own challenges. (*Matthew* 6:34)

The ants teach me to get on with the job and to be a good team-player. I suppose that, in 'ant' terms, my church is my spiritual 'colony'. How much real use to it am I? Have I become one of its leading 'postponers'? Have I joined that 'yes-it-needs-to-be-done-but-let's-talk-about-it-at-the-next-meeting' brigade? Have I fallen into the trap of accepting never-ending planning as a substitute for real action? When active fellow-Christians need my encouragement, am I one of my church's complainers or one of its confirmers? "Go to the ant thou sluggard!"

TODAY'S RESOLVE

Today, I will not be a sluggard.

"Lord, help me not to put off things- to make that call, send that e-mail, and write that letter of encouragement without delay. Amen!"

DAY SIX

6. BETTER THE DEVIL YOU KNOW

Proverbs 6:12-19

Key verse:-6:12-13 "Worthless liars go around winking and giving signals to deceive others"

The 'worthless liar' is no likeable rogue. He is sneaky and underhand. If the Sluggard is *Proverbs'* clown, this man is its villain. I think that the modern translation hides the bluntness of the original which calls him 'a son of Belial' – a name which Paul uses for Satan himself (*II Corinthians*. 6:15). To me, 'the worthless liar' is a case-study designed to unmask the nature of evil and to warn me of things I must never forget. I may not picture the Devil as a mediaeval horned horror but I am sure that there is an evil power at work in the world resisting all that I hold dear and that that power has identifiable characteristics.

Firstly, the devil is a liar. In the wilderness, Jesus exposes Satan as the greatest confidence-trickster of all time. He offers Jesus such an attractive proposition, "II will give you the whole world if you will bow down and worship me" (*Matthew* 4:9). But the deal is a fraud. Satan is offering to 'fence' stolen goods and I must always work on the assumption that anything evil says is a lie. Temptations only work when I allow myself to be 'conned' into believing that I'll be happier if I surrender to them.

Next, the devil is 'a joker'. Evil appears as harmless fun -the 'worthless liar goes around winking and giving signals to deceive others'. What a vivid picture! While seducing his victims, the devil winks knowingly at his supporters and gestures to them behind his back. What 'a card' he is! He's the life and soul of any party. Always good for a laugh! Humour is both one of God's greatest gifts and one of the devil's cruellest weapons. Satan urges me to believe that anything –foul-mouthed comedy, cruel satire, sexual innuendo – is acceptable providing that it is thought 'funny'. If I think otherwise, I am a narrow-minded bigot.

Finally, the devil is proactive. The 'son of Belial' is 'always thinking up something evil to stir up trouble'. In a nutshell – he is always looking for somebody to do his dirty work and, if I fall for his lies, he will use me to entrap others. Evil is a communicable disease, spreading its contagion by personal contact and it wants to use me as 'a carrier'. I must beware! There is much to be said for the old adage, "Better the devil you know"!

TODAY'S RESOLVE

Today, I will be spiritually alert.

"Lord, make me remember how 'temptable' I am and save me from being used to cause harm to others – even under the guise of harmless fun. Amen!"

7. PLAYING WITH FIRE

Proverbs 6:20-29

Key verse:-6:27 "If you carry burning coals, you burn your clothes'

I see a picture. A Palestinian, who carries glowing coals in a pot to light his fire, must expect at least a few scorch-marks on his long, flowing clothes, and maybe something much worse. The Wise Man says that sexual indulgence is like that. It leaves its mark. He describes how a man's thoughtless flirtation brings him personal disaster, disgraces his family, ruins a marriage and plunges an entire community into conflict. It is certainly a timely warning for our society. There is a price to be paid for regarding sex as entertainment and pornography as harmless indulgence.

However, I have a feeling that the principle has wider applications. In *Ecclesiasticus* (13:1), where I find a parallel idea – "He who touches pitch will be defiled". 'Defiled' means 'stuck to my hand'. In other words, if I handle anything evil, no matter how fleetingly, it will 'stick to my hand'. I find that very uncomfortable. How often have I said, "Well, just this once" or "It won't matter this time"? But it *does* matter! Holding the fire of temptation, even briefly, is enough to scorch and weaken me.

I have another idea. Why not apply this principle *positively*? Surely, it must also work if I carry the fire of faith. Embracing *good* must leave its mark on me just as much as embracing *evil*. I remember how John Wesley described the moment when divine assurance flooded his soul. He said, "I felt my heart strangely warmed". As a child, he was 'plucked as a brand' from his father's burning rectory but now he was aglow with love and joy, ready to carry the gospel fire to others.

I realise that, whatever 'fire' I choose to carry affects both me and other people. John Donne was right, "No man is an island entire unto itself". Our lives are intimately intertwined. If I flirt with evil, others too may be weakened. However, if they see me carrying the fire of faith, they too may be 'warmed'. Either way, it's a sobering thought that today; my influence may make somebody better or worse.

TODAY'S RESOLVE

Today, I will remember that I may be playing with fire.

"Lord, save me from doing or saying anything that may make others think that evil is acceptable. Amen!"

DAY EIGHT

8. THE BUNDLE OF LIFE

Proverbs 8:32-36

Key verses:-8:35-36 "By finding me, you find life..But if you hate me, you are in love with death."

I like this picture of Wisdom as a noble lady dispensing bounty to those around her but I notice that her generosity has a sting in its tail. "You are free to accept or reject my presents," she says", but remember that they are not just optional trinkets; they are matters of life and death."

I see from the commentaries that the Wise Man generally seems uncertain about survival after death, so, when he says that those who find Wisdom, 'find life', he means that the two go hand-in-hand in *this* world. Those who live life in God's way are the people who are *really alive!* This sounds fine but, if it's true, why do so many people with no time for God still seem to have such a great time? It is still raises questions in my mind. They don't look 'dead' to me! Perhaps appearances are deceptive.

Maybe the clue lies in what the Wise Man says about *finding* life. In other words, the meaning of life doesn't automatically fall into my lap. I have to look for it. How often I have read Job's solemn words at funerals, (always in the *KJV* version of course) "The Lord gave and the Lord has taken away; blessed be the name of the Lord. (1:21) They state a basic truth. I can buy many things but 'life' is not one of them.

Life is more than mere respiration. Life is God's supreme, undeserved present to me. I love the classical version of Abigail's words to David, "The life of my Lord shall be bound in the bundle of life with the Lord your God" (*I Samuel.* 25: 29). What a wonderful description! Life is a bundle of rich gifts, experiences and relationships which God gives me to enjoy for his glory. Missing out on that is like being given a precious Stradivarius violin but never bothering to learn to play it.

I understand better now what Jesus meant when he said that, through him, I "might have life in all its fullness." (*John* 10:10). He wasn't just talking about the after-life. He came to show me how to enjoy God's gift of life here and now. That is a wonderfully liberating idea. The Wise Man is right. There has to be a sort of spiritual 'deadness' about those who reject God because they never really discover what life is all about. They never completely open the bundle of life and take out all its treasures.

TODAY'S RESOLVE

Today, I will value the Bundle of Life.

"Dear Lord, help me to value every experience and encounter today and, when night comes, I will thank you for the rich gift of life. Amen!"

9. PILLARS

Proverbs 9:1-9

Key verse:-9:1 "Wisdom has built its house with its seven columns"

Scholars have had a field-day trying to sort out its meaning. The pillars or columns have been identified with everything from Sennacherib's temple to the seven days of creation and the seven heavenly bodies. However, I think that, since seven is the perfect number, it just means that Lady Wisdom's palace is built on perfect, strong foundations. This has made me think about strong pillars. What would I say are the seven 'strong pillars' of my life as a Christian? I'll choose four for today and save the rest for tomorrow.

BELIEF IN GOD: Everybody must decide for themselves whether or not God exists. Either way, it must be guesswork because our little minds can't prove the answer. Atheists need just as much 'faith' as believers! Although trying to imagine God blows my mind, long ago, on the basis of probabilities, I deliberately chose to be a believer and, having tested it for many years, I still find that it makes the best sense. In spite of having occasional spiritual 'off days', my first strong pillar remains my conviction that everything relates to God.

TRUST IN GOD: I live life on the assumption that God is good and can be trusted. Seeing life through the lens of faith, experience has taught me that

God is reliable so that I usually manage to "live by faith and not by what we see" (*II Corinthians.* 5:7). However, to be honest, there are times when the pillar wobbles and I am ashamed of just how untrusting I can be. At such times, I depend heavily on my third pillar.

THE AUTHORITY OF JESUS: Although I honour other faiths, I declare that, as a Christian, it is my attitude to Jesus that makes me distinctive. Others may respect and venerate him but, for me, he is God in understandable human form, a Saviour whose teaching has divine authority and is totally prescriptive for my life. I believe that, when I see Jesus, I see what God is like.

THE REALITY OF THE HOLY SPIRIT: Jesus' last earthly promise was that he would help me to follow him "The Holy Spirit will come upon you and give you power" (*Acts* 1:8) I know that the spiritual power of Jesus has invaded my life. What my mind tells me about God has become an experienced reality within me. There are my first four 'pillars'.

TODAY'S RESOLVE

Today, I will not apologize for my Christian faith.

"My Lord and my God, remind me that my faith in you carries the validity of careful thought and long personal experience. Help me to share it simply and winsomely with others. Amen!"

DAY TEN

10. MORE PILLARS

Proverbs 9:1-9

Key verse:-9:1 "Wisdom has built its house with its seven columns"

Today, I'll choose my remaining 'strong pillars'.

THE DISCIPLINE OF PRAYER. Jesus has shown me the wonderful simplicity of prayer as a conversation with my heavenly Father. So I fervently believe that my prayer changes things, even though I am not always sure how it works. In a very humbling way, God uses my prayer as a door through which I can pass to stand with him in any given situation. Sadly, I do not always feel like praying and some experts tell me just to give up at such times. But that does not work for me. I find that I do better if I observe the *discipline* of prayer, whether or not I'm in the mood. My regular prayer-times are strong pillars which hold me steady even when I am waiting for the joy of prayer to return.

THE IMPORTANCE OF FELLOWSHIP. I'm glad that Jesus chose his group of young men to travel together to show that his disciples are not always intended to be lone pilgrims. For as long as I can remember, the Church has been a strong pillar of my life, even when I have despaired of it (and *vice versa!*). Like all families, it has its ups and downs but it is still my spiritual family and I cherish it. How much I have received from fellow-Christians! It has not just been memorable spiritual high-points which have blessed me

29

but the routines of ordinary church life – the inspiration of worship, the intimacy of prayer, the insights of study and the fun of social events. Such fellowship must be counted as one of my strong pillars.

THE PRINCIPLE OF GROWTH. I'm not sure how this has pushed itself in to take the last place but it is here and I must respect it. The Bible's picture of the Christian life is one of growth development and that is very important to me. For many years, I have kept a detailed journal of my daily happenings and I think I understand why. Each day, no matter how routine or ordinary, is a voyage of discovery and, when it ends, I am a changed person. Just as thousands of my physical cells have been replaced, so my soul will have been changed by hundreds of different thoughts and experiences. This is my seventh pillar – the belief that the Christian life is dynamic not static. In this earthly life, I am never the finished article. The Holy Spirit is always working on me, removing the dents, polishing the dullness's and remoulding the imperfections – of which there are there are so many.

TODAY'S RESOLVE

Today, I will make today a positive experience of God.

"Lord Jesus, as you lead me into the adventure of today, let me come to its end knowing that you have changed me for the better. Amen!"

DAY ELEVEN

11. THE ULTIMATE REVERENCE

Proverbs 9:10-18

Key verse:-9:10 "Respect and obey the Lord! This is the beginning of wisdom"

In my mind's eye, I can still see it - a floridly-framed text on the Sunday School wall. *The fear of the Lord is the beginning of wisdom.* Even then, I thought it was odd that I should be told to be afraid of God but I supposed that grown-ups must know best. Of course, I now translate 'fear' as 'reverence' – holding God in deepest respect- but, although it sets the right tone, it still confronts me with an uncomfortable question. "If I am a divine creation and not a piece of accidental cosmic flotsam, where does my Creator stand in my life? Do I hold him in *deepest respect* as the ultimate reality in everything I do?"

I'm the first to admit that I can be a rotten Christian but sometimes I get things right and, when I *do,* why should I pretend that I haven't? I remember Ignatius Loyola's sensible warning that, "the devil tries to draw us into false and noxious humility". I think that this is something that I *have* got right. I *do* believe that I am a divine creation and that God's place is at the centre of my life. That is what gives direction to everything I do.

Coincidentally, I have just been reading about how Lord Kelvin's brilliant use of magnets, saved the first iron ships when their metal distorted their

31

compass-readings and sent them wildly off course. There are times when that is my story too. My commitment to God veers off course and, when that happens, it is my conviction that God is like Jesus that works like Kelvin's magnets and sets me voyaging again. His life is my navigation chart.

I think that that's what the Wise Man is getting at here. 'Respecting God' means living a God-controlled life and accepting his divine direction for daily life. It is that that makes me 'wise' and, without it, I can never become truly skilled at the business of living. However, I don't always find God's guidance clear and it is a great comfort to learn that even the great saints have had that problem. I notice that the Bible speaks more than fifty times of 'waiting for God' and perhaps that's the clue. If I really 'respect' God, I will trust not only his direction but his timing too. When that becomes hard, I take comfort from the Psalmist's testimony "I patiently waited, Lord...you listened...let me stand on a rock.... and gave me a new song". (*Psalms* 40:1-3)

TODAY'S RESOLVE

Today, I will take seriously my place in God's plans.

"O Lord, you created me for a purpose, teach me that your plans and your times are best and give me patience to understand them. Amen!"

DAY TWELVE

12. SILENCE IS GOLDEN

Proverbs 10:1-14

Key verse:-10:14 "Foolish talk will soon destroy you"

Curiosity has made me look up 'tongue' in my Bible concordance. I have found almost a hundred references to it - mostly in *Proverbs* and mostly hostile. The tongue is called everything from a 'sword' and a 'scourge' to 'a raging fire' and 'a deadly poison' – quite a reputation for such a little organ of the body! Digging deeper, I have discovered three major charges against the tongue – and I've just thought up three great words for them!

Firstly, the tongue is *mendacious* (what my Grandmother called 'a fine-Sunday-go-to-meeting word' for *lying*) Why does that make me feel uncomfortable? I hope that I have outgrown telling out-and-out lies or almost all those little 'half-truths' which are really 'half-lies'. In fact, I think that I am doing well until I remember that Jesus requires a 100% success-rate. "When you make a promise, say only 'Yes' or 'No'," he says and then he adds (pointing to my 'half-truths'?) "Anything else comes from the devil." (*Matthew* 5:37) There's a thought – in the devil's hands, my unguarded half-truths can be more damaging than fully-grown lies!

Secondly, the tongue is *manipulative*- a trouble maker. I like *The Living Bible's* paraphrase, '*Only a fool*

33

blurts out everything he knows – that only leads to trouble. 'The text actually means that the tongue "causes imminent ruin". Its effects are immediate. A word once spoken has a life and power of its own. No matter how much I apologise afterwards, damaging words can never be unsaid. I still shudder when I remember times when I have forgotten that! It is the tongue's *immediate* influence that makes it so good at manipulating people. To be honest, what eloquent dictators have done with entire nations, I have often been tempted to do on a smaller scale with individuals.

Thirdly, the tongue is *malicious* - a violent bully. Few sayings are more stupid than, "Sticks and stones may break my bones but calling names won't hurt me". Words can leave invisible wounds, deeper and more long-lasting than any physical cuts and bruises. I seem to remember that it was Blaise Pascal who said that, "hot words scorch people" and, sadly, I can think of a few people I have 'scorched' in my time. When I misuse my tongue, it 'destroys' me as much as its victim. I must take a deep breath before speaking.

TODAY'S RESOLVE

Today, I will really try to think before I speak, especially when I am under pressure.

"Lord, today I may not have time to 'count to ten' before I speak. Save me from the sins of the tongue. May I say nothing untrue, scheming or hurtful. Use my tongue to encourage and bless. Amen!"

13. A BLESSING TO MYSELF

Proverbs 11: 15-23

Key verse:-11:17 "Kindness is rewarded-but if you are cruel you hurt yourself".

I feel I ought not to expect a reward for doing what is right but the proverb says that that is a gracious bi-product of being kind to others. The *KJV* makes this clearer when it says; *The merciful man does good for his own soul.* I'm intrigued to see that 'kindness' translates that lovely Hebrew word *hesed* which means God's undeserved, steadfast love for me. What an amazing idea! I am a blessing to myself when I treat others as God treats me. It has made me think about some of those blessings.

Being kind makes me feel happy. When I act like God, I am nourished by a wonderful sense of 'doing the right thing'. It is like listening to an orchestra tuning up before a concert. Gradually all the discords disappear and there is perfect harmony. When I serve others, I feel that my life is in tune with God. Deep down, I know that being true to God is also being true to myself and that makes me happy.

Next, I think that being kind has a cumulative effect. Each time I am kind, kindness grows stronger within me. Frankly, sometime I find it very hard to be kind but, if I can be kind even on those occasions, I will grow a little better at loving people. I have often quoted Charles Reade's maxim, "Sow an act and you reap a habit. Sow a habit and you reap a character". It's true. For good or ill, my habits eventually become part of my personality. Perhaps, one day, the Holy Spirit will make being kind my instinctive reaction to *every* situation. It will be part of 'understanding what Christ is thinking' (*I Corinthians* 2:16)

Then, I realise that kindness is an education for me. When I'm challenged to be kind, I learn a lot about myself and about other people. I learn both how kindness can transform lives and I learn the more difficult lesson that kindness doesn't always work miracles. Needy people are not necessarily nice people! Gradually I hope to stop being hyper-sensitive about ingratitude. Becoming angry when my kindness is rejected or mocked is so unlike 'the mind of Christ'. Perhaps most important of all, being kind teaches me about God. I begin to understand the inexhaustible riches of his kindness to me and I catch a glimpse – just a glimpse- of what it means to be a loving God.

TODAY'S RESOLVE

Today, I will not be unkind to anybody in any way.

"Kindly Lord, save me from being unkind simply because I am stupid or insensitive. Today, let me touch lives with your kindness. Amen!"

DAY FOURTEEN

14. MONEY! MONEY! MONEY!

Proverbs 11:24-28

Key verse:-11:24 "Sometimes you can become rich by being generous or poor by being greedy."

The Bible talks so much about money that I have just given up trying to count the references. ABBA's famous hit *Money! Money! Money!* describes perfectly its fascination and lure. I need to think carefully about money. In itself, it may be neutral but its power to buy and sell makes it very important.

Paul was right to warn me that, *the love of money causes all kinds of trouble* (*I Timothy* 6:10) because 'loving' money is nothing less than a lust for some sort of power. However, if money represents power, God can also use the power of money in his service and, if I allow him to use my money, then I will be blessed too. But how?

It is here that I am remembering just how much I admire John Wesley's common sense approach to the Christian's use of money. In his sermon, *On The Use of Money,* after reminding me to pay my taxes and to avoid fraud, he gives me three excellent pieces of advice. I have no problem with the first two, "Gain all you can" (there's no shame in honest wealth) and "save all you can" (it's wise to provide for one's future).

However, the third piece of advice – "Give all you can"- raises a question in my mind. "Do I have to give all I can to everybody?" My difficulty is that people don't fall into two neat categories - selfish, evil people and God-serving good ones. I know many unbelievers who use their money wisely and respond to charities and I know many 'good' people who are downright 'stingy'. So what is distinctive about my giving *as a Christian?*

Jesus says that it is the *second* mile of service which is the distinctive mark of his followers. They have an extra-positive attitude towards generosity which often seems reckless in the eyes of the world. The glorious irrationality of the man giving away his tunic *and* his cloak, the widow donating her last 'mite' and the woman pouring out her precious ointment; none of them make any earthly sense but they all draw Christ's special praise. So it means that, *as a Christian,* I must not only be particularly aware of my money's power but I must actively look for opportunities to be generous. In the divine economy, it makes real sense but it's hard!

TODAY'S RESOLVE

Today, I will look for at least one opportunity to be generous.

"Lord, thank you for giving me so much. Give me an opportunity today to imitate your divine generosity and to do it with joy. Amen!"

15. R.S.P.C.A.

Proverbs 12:5-10

Key verse:-12:10 "Good people are kind to their animals but a mean person is cruel".

Why am I so surprised to find a proverb about being kind to animals? *Genesis* says that they are part of God's 'good' creation and the Bible is a menagerie of all kinds of creatures from lions to maggots. As the hymn says, "The Lord God made them all" and he is the often unacknowledged divine patron of the R.S.P.C.A. and all other societies for the welfare of animals.

Ever since I was given my first rabbit, pets have brought me wonderful joy. Unlike the Wise Man, I can never fully know the profound, mystical bond that exists between farmers and their stock but I can see the truth behind these words. The way that I treat animals reveals whether or not I am genuinely 'a good person' because animals are in my power. George Eliot was right, "Animals are such agreeable friends... they ask no questions, they pass no criticisms."

I try to look at other translations and, when I did, I was really puzzled by other versions of the second part of this problem. For instance, the *NIV* reads, *But the kindest acts of the wicked are cruel*. How can kindness be cruel? I suppose that the Wise Man is carrying the issue of genuineness a stage further. What appears outwardly to be a kindly act can be counterfeit, a clever deception. Ultimately, whatever wicked, mean people do, will be tainted by selfishness and sin.

I have seen this principle in action! I have lived in countries where, every day, state-controlled television has trumpeted the 'kindness' of dictators but their 'kindness' has been deceptively manipulative and conditional. Woe betide anybody who got in their way! It was one big fraud; the real test of my kindness is how I treat creatures which cannot stop me being cruel to them.

The idea that kindness to animals is an indicator of genuine goodness is thought-provoking, especially when expanded to include all creation. Jesus spoke with such affection of plants and animals and he clearly expected his followers to respect and protect God's creation. I cannot, single-handed, stop cruelty to animals, save endangered species, cure the throw-away society or prevent global warming but I can do more for the 'fight for kindness' than I am doing at present. As a Christian, I have a responsibility to improve my support for every 'green' project.

TODAY'S RESOLVE

Today, I will consciously and actively respect God's creation.

"Lord, my Creator, show me practical ways to befriend your planet and give me the will to act upon them. Amen!"

16. MY WORD IS MY BOND

Proverbs 12:16-22

Key verse:-12:22 "The Lord hates every liar but he is the friend of all who can be trusted".

Promise is such a noble word! From the Latin 'to send forth', it's a statement of what *will* happen, a confident expectation. It makes me think of pictures of the annual New Forest horse-sales, where dealers haggle fiercely over the price of the animals but, once agreed; they strike palms together and shake hands. They 'strike a deal'. There's no need for signed papers or witnessed agreements. They are not liars. Their word is their bond. That's the kind of person to whom God 'is a friend'.

I can't help contrasting this with the spurious promises that bombard us every day – easy finance, unbelievable holidays, 'reliable' house-repairs, incredible investments and life-changing cosmetics. The whole idea of trust seems to be under attack. Double standards are rife. What is 'disgraceful' when it is done to me becomes 'fair game' when I do it to other people. This is very dangerous. You can't build a society on broken promises. It spawns the terrible cynicism with which so many people today regard politicians, policemen, church leaders and anybody in authority. When people can't trust one another, eventually their community implodes.

The proverb makes me realise that the issue is as much theological as sociological. It is *God* who delights in kept promises and abhors broken one. Honesty is derived from the very nature of God himself. The Bible is packed with divine promises from a God who never breaks his word. I see Jesus as the living proof of this. The Father keeps his promises even at the cost of his own Son's humiliation and murder. Jesus is both the proof of God's integrity and the channel through which I myself receive 'great and marvellous promises' (*II Peter* 1:4 cf. *II Corinthians* 1:20)

The practical effect of this is that I cannot follow such a Lord with broken promises, half-fulfilled vows and crafty evasions. I wonder if I *always* reflect God's integrity in my dealings with other people. If God keeps his promises to me, God expects me to keep my promises to other people and 'hates' it when I don't. I need to think more carefully about God's promises – and mine!

TODAY'S RESOLVE

Today, I will claim God's promises and be careful to keep my own.

"Lord, you have kept so many wonderful promises to me in my life, save me today from making promises that I cannot keep. Amen!"

17. GRIST TO THE MILL

Proverbs 12:23-28

Key verse:-12:27 "Anyone too lazy to cook will starve but a hard worker is a valuable treasure"

This is another of those occasions when the *CEB* catches the general meaning of a difficult verse but I like the *NIV* which says, "The lazy man does not roast his game but the diligent man prizes his possessions." The Lazy Man is another of *Proverbs'* repertory company of players. He lives a life of unfulfilled good intentions. I'm sure that he fully intended to prepare that 'kill' for his table but he never quite got around to it. I know that I should do better than he does but, as I've already confessed, there's a bit of the Lazy Man in me. I have to fight against putting off difficult or uninteresting tasks and I need to learn from the second character in the proverb – 'the diligent man'.

He has two virtues that I covet. Firstly, he really lives by Horace's maxim *Seize the day!* He lives in the here and now, singing with the Psalmist, "This day belongs to the Lord! Let's celebrate and be glad today." (*Psalms* 118:24) I need to remember Jesus' warning about being so focussed upon the uncertainties of the future that I squander the opportunities of the present. (*Matthew* 6:34)

This positive approach leads to the 'diligent man's' second admirable quality. As *The Living Bible* brilliantly paraphrases it, he "makes good use of everything he finds." The 'diligent man' enters each 'today' positively, looking for anything that he can use. This reminded me of, "All's grist to my mill', I looked it up and found that 'grist' was the amount of corn that could be ground at any one time. So the saying means, "I can turn everything to my advantage"   As a Christian that is what I can do with every 'today'. God can transmute every encounter and every experience into the gold of usefulness. Brother Lawrence insisted that he found the presence of God 'as much when scouring pans in the kitchen as when kneeling before the Blessed Sacrament.'

It reminds me of visiting an exhibition of lovely sculptures made from driftwood. I was amazed by the way that the artist had taken wooden waste and made it beautiful. All it needed was his eye and skill to use what others would have thrown away. Isn't that what the Spirit can do for me? He can take and use even the flotsam and jetsam of life. In his hands, nothing that happens to me is rubbish.

TODAY'S RESOLVE

Today, I will take "Seize the day!" as my guide.

"Lord, take the energy I waste on wishing that things were different and harness it for your glory. Amen!"

18. STAY FOCUSSED

Proverbs 13:14-22

Key verse:-13:19 "It's a good feeling to get what you want, but only a stupid fool hates to turn from evil."

Sitting in a church in the United States, I heard Christian youth-counsellor tell a group of teenagers. "You can be whatever you want to be, but you must stay focussed, focussed, focussed!" Life was presented as a supermarket of choices in which the young people could wander with unlimited credit-cards. The really successful people are those who plan for their future and march relentlessly towards it – and how we love winners! But the counsellor's words worried me then and they still do.

They sound to me like a Winners' Charter. But what about the people who 'stay focussed' all their lives but never achieve their dreams? What about the people to whom life has dealt a crippling hand of illness and deprivation? What about the two-thirds of the human race that has virtually no choices at all, who are so abjectly poor that they can 'focus' simply on staying alive?

However, today's proverb raises another doubt in my mind. What happens if I succeed in staying focussed but on the wrong things? As the proverb says, I love it when my plans work out but what if I become so obsessed with them that I can't see when they are wrong? Then, like the 'stupid fool', I will stay focussed on them but with baleful results. Sadly, I can speak from experience!

This idea of focussing on a plan for life is such a puzzle and, trying to sort it out always brings the same words to my mind –"Looking to Jesus, the pioneer and perfecter of our faith" (*Hebrews* 12:2) (I still prefer the older version). This is surely the clue I need. If I stay focussed on the person and teaching of Jesus, he will guide my plan for life because I'm here as part of *God's* plan. It's not a matter of being whatever *I* want to do but of being what *He* wants me to do.

I often think that God's plans for me are like the shining workings of my grandfather's pocket-watch. He would open its case and show me how the small and large cogs all meshed together to keep perfect time. The 'big cog' –major life-changing events which God puts into my life- will only function properly if I pay attention to the 'little cog'- the minor experiences of daily living. They must work together. If I *focus* on being obedient in small things, I will be ready to embrace the large ones.

TODAY'S RESOLVE

Today, I will focus on the little cogs.

"Lord make me faithful in little things today so that I can stay focussed on all your plans for my life. Amen!"

DAY NINETEEN

19. ON WITH THE MOTLEY!

Proverbs 14:6-14

Key verse:-14:13 "Sorrow may hide behind laughter and happiness may end in sorrow".

This has set me thinking about laughter and I've checked a half-remembered quotation from the essayist William Hazlett. "Man is the only animal that laughs and weeps, for he is the only animal that is struck by the difference between what things are and what they might have been." Certainly, no other animal uses laughter so subtly. The same physiological phenomenon has so many nuances. It can be cruel or kind – everything from chuckles of delight to sneers of sadistic mockery. It can express sheer joy, celebrate the ridiculous, hide embarrassment or even, as the Wise Man says, it can be a mask for grief.

To my shame, I'm not an opera-lover but even I am moved by that moment in *Pagliacci* when the broken-hearted clown sings, *On with the motley,* dons his ridiculous clothes and goes out to caper for the crowd. His antics and garb hide his grief from the onlookers. Most people, at some time in their lives, empathise with the old song, "laughing on the outside but crying on the inside'. Why? Why do people laugh to hide a heavy heart?

This proverb makes me realise that, when I've been privileged to sit with sad people, their motives for laughter have been very complex. They have used it to protect themselves, both from being destroyed by their grief and from being smothered by others' sympathy. They have used laughter kindly to ease sympathisers' embarrassment. It has been their way of saying, "Don't worry too much about me. You see I can still smile."

On the other hand, their laughter has sometimes been more bitter than benevolent. It has had a sharp edge which says, "Life is a sick joke – and the joke's on me!" I once read that the *Book of Job* has almost more references to laughter than any other book of the Bible. If it's true, it must be said that most of them are soaked in irony.

Jesus teaches me not to depend on first impressions. He saw a rock in vacillating Simon, generosity in miserly Zacchaeus and purity in the adulteress. How uncomfortably this compares with my tendency to jump to conclusions about others. In particular, I need to 'read' their laughter, especially since it may be an SOS sent out to those sensitive enough to hear and respond.

TODAY'S RESOLVE

Today, I will take laughter seriously.

"Lord, thank you for the gift of laughter. Help me to realise the effect of my own laughter and to respond rightly to the signals being sent out by the laughter of others. Amen!"

DAY TWENTY

20. RELAXED CHRISTIANS

Proverbs 14:29-35

Key verse:-14:30 "It's healthy to be content but envy can eat you up"

Stress is the scourge of contemporary western society and 'stress management' is big business. Insightfully, the Wise Man identifies envy as a prime cause of stress. He warns that there is a kind of congenital dissatisfaction with one's lot which 'eats up' enjoyment of life. Instead of appreciating what they already have, people pine for what others possess. Am I absolutely innocent? There are times when I *do* envy other people's gifts and possessions. Wanting things can be my Achilles' heel. I need to remember the good advice, "Don't fall in love with money. Be satisfied with what you have." (*Hebrews*13:5)

This raises another question for me. For instance, being a Christian doesn't exempt me from essential, everyday 'normal' stress but there are times when my stress-level can get out of hand. Is it blasphemous to think that Jesus himself experienced such stress? How else do I explain his need to seek solitude in the wilderness, the tears in the Garden of Gethsemane or the Cry of Dereliction on the cross? Blasphemous or not, when I am stressed, I like to think that my Wonderful Counsellor knows how I am feeling. He knows that, sometimes, I have to confront stressful situations without flinching but he also knows that I can't live with stress forever. I have to learn to relax, to slacken life's bow-string. God had good reason for building the *Sabbath* principle into the very fabric of creation (*Genesis* 2:2f.) and there are times when Jesus tells me to "Come apart and rest awhile". (*Mark* 7:22, *Luke* 12:5)

But there is a nagging thought at the back of my mind. Surely, I ought to be working hard for God all the time! Am I the only Christian who finds that sometimes my faith actually adds to my stress? The stern sense of duty that flows in my Protestant veins confuses faith with frenzied activity and then wraps them both in guilt. "If you were a *real* Christian", I scold myself, you would do this and you wouldn't do that!" I'm sure God does not intend me to live a life of perpetual guilty stress. At such times I need to get a theological grip and remember that I'm saved by grace and not good works and that Jesus told me to 'love myself', offering rest to the 'heavy laden' not bigger burdens. He alone can give me that 'relaxed attitude' which shows my non-Christian friends that it is possible to live with stress without being destroyed by it.

TODAY'S RESOLVE

Today, I will confront and control my stress.

"Loving Lord, alert me when my stress-level is climbing dangerously and show me how to relax and restore equilibrium. Amen!"

DAY TWENTY-ONE

21. BEING GRUNTLED

Proverbs 15:1-10

Key verse:-15:4 "Kind words are good medicine but deceitful words can really hurt"

It wasn't until I led that week-long silent retreat for clergy that I realised just how many unnecessary words I use to lubricate the business of everyday living. The Wise Man is making me think afresh about the words I use - both what I say and how I say it. I like the idea that there are two sorts of speaking – 'kind' and 'deceitful'.

My first Christian ancestors virtually Invented kindness and claimed it as a gift of the Spirit (*II Corinthians* 6:6). Their world regarded gentleness as weakness but they saw that only the genuinely strong can be 'kind'. Cruelty is a product of fear and 'kind' people must overcome their fear and have respect for others. St. Francis de Sales (one of my favourite saints) said, "Nothing is so strong as gentleness, nothing so gentle as real strength."

I also need to remember that the way I speak matters almost as much as what I say. When I am hurried or thoughtless, I sometimes forget that my tone of voice can change the whole meaning of my words. I only have to think of the number of different ways that I can say the simple word 'yes to see the danger. Just by changing my tone, I can make it mean anything from

51

joyful acceptance to reluctant refusal, I need to be careful. Saying the right things in the right way truly is 'good medicine'.

Seeing that *The Living Bible* interprets 'deceitful' as 'grumbling' has made me realise that there is, indeed, a kind of grumbling that combines deceit with complaint. I love Wodehouse's splendid sentence in *Curse of the Woosters,* "I could see that, if not actually disgruntled, he was far from being gruntled". Surely 'being gruntled' is the Wise Man's 'deceitful grumbling'! It does not complain honestly but carps and mutters under its breath. It is what the Bible calls 'murmuring'- the intermittent grumbling of the Israelites against Moses and Aaron and the aggrieved mutterings of the Greek widows in the early church (*Exodus* 16:2, *Acts* 6:1

I realise that 'underground' grumbling 'really hurts'. It is spiritual dry-rot in a church, sapping its leaders' confidence and destroying congregations by stealth. Church leaders work is hard enough without my sniping whenever I disagree with them. If I can replace being 'far from gruntled' with words of confidence, encouragement and hope, what a blessing I will be!

TODAY'S RESOLVE

Today, I will be 'gruntled' and I will speak kindly.

"Lord Jesus, give me your genuine gentleness, so that I encourage the people I meet instead of criticising them. Amen!"

22. PLANNING AND TRUSTING

Proverbs 16:1-9

Key verse:-16:9 "We make our own plans, but the Lord decides where we will go".

I am remembering how annoyed I was with three 'missionaries' who arrived uninvited in our community, claiming to 'walk entirely by faith'. They told a peasant congregation that they should be fed and housed because that was the command of 'the God who never fails'. I resented the exploitation of those poor Christians under the guise of 'faith'. The three men were blackmailing those people into showing their generosity but, even worse, they were blackmailing God into proving his reliability. 'Living by faith' does not mean not bothering to make sensible plans

However, I don't find it easy to walk the tight-rope slung between trusting God and accepting responsibility for my own life. It can't be right for me to pray for guidance and then organize my life without God but it seems just as wrong to sit back and leave everything to him. How far ought I to plan ahead? The Wise Man tells me that I should be 'prudent'. It is one of his favourite words; almost half the Bible's references to 'prudence' occur in *Proverbs*. It is a solid, sensible word meaning careful living in the present and wise provision for the future. It was while thinking about this that I stumbled on a little saying of St. Ambrose, "No man is prudent who is ignorant of God" and, if he's right, there is nothing wrong about making plans, providing that I put God in charge of the process.

53

Although, outwardly, my decisions may look exactly like those of unbelievers, the Wise Man insists that they are basically different because I count on the Lord 'decide where I will go'. Faith is the secret ingredient in my planning. I take seriously Jesus' words that "the very hairs of my head are numbered" (*Matthew* 10:30). I honestly believe that the God who loves me like that finds many different ways to influence my life.

Sometimes, God changes my plans by fertilizing them with other people's ideas or he uses unforeseen events or gives me 'unexpected revelations'. God doesn't always make things easier for me but God uses everything for my blessing. God never just leaves me at the mercy of my own inadequate planning. On his deathbed, John Wesley declared, "The best of all is, God is with us" – and, since dying people don't waste their breath, I believe him!

TODAY'S RESOLVE

Today, I will take God's continual presence seriously.

"Loving Lord, I ask you to take control of my life today, so that you may use everything that happens to change and mould me. Amen!"

23. CONTEMPT ON ALL MY PRIDE

Proverbs 16:10-23

**Key verses:-16:17-18 "God's people
...watch where they go. Too much pride
will destroy you"**

In its more familiar form, "Pride goes before a fall" this must be the best-known and most misquoted of all proverbs, muttered smugly whenever the arrogant 'get their come-uppance'. However, for the Wise Man, it is no joke and the fierceness of his warning has made me look back at some of his other references to pride. Three of them in particular have made me think.

Earlier in the same chapter, he says, "The Lord doesn't like anyone who is conceited" (16:5) He warns me that **pride ruins my relationship with God.** It tempts me to manage without Him. I'm just like Adam in the garden, thinking that I can be godlike. I need to be very careful because pride can alienate me from God. D.L. Moody once said that, "God sends no one away empty except those who are full of themselves". I don't want that to happen to me!

Next, I turned to 13:10 and read, "Too much pride causes trouble". By creating disharmony, **pride ruins my relationship with other people.** Isn't pride subtle? It exploits the fact that, sometimes, I *am* right and it makes me think that, therefore, I must *always* be right. I begin to confuse defending a principle with defending my own *ego.* "Does it *really* matter if I *am* proved right?" Which is more important, winning this argument or maintaining this relationship?

Early in Chapter Eleven, there are some uncomfortable words. "Too much pride can put you to shame." (11:2) Pride is the archetypal sin and it not only ruins my relationship with God and other people, it even **ruins my relationship with *myself*.** It makes me lose the ability to see myself as I really am and I begin to minimize my weaknesses and maximize my virtues. This sort of distorting mirror does me no favours. Eventually, the truth will catch up with me and I will be ashamed of my stupidity. I must walk warily through the minefield of pride, following in the footsteps of Jesus who was, "humble, obeyed God and even died on a cross". (*Philippians* 2:8) When tempted to flirt with pride, I only need to sing with Isaac Watts, *When I survey the wondrous Cross on which the Prince of Glory died, my richest gain I count but loss and pour contempt on all my pride.*

TODAY'S RESOLVE

Today, I will watch pride like a hawk.

"Humble Lord, you know how vulnerable I am. Show me my strengths and weaknesses, so that my pride doesn't exaggerate either. Amen!"

56

DAY TWENTY-FOUR

24. CLOSING THE FLOOD-GATES

Proverbs 17:7-16

Key verse:-17:14 "The start of an argument is like a water leak- so stop it before real trouble breaks out."

I'm not normally a confrontational sort of person with a 'short fuse', however, I still have to be careful when I disagree with other people. Quarrels can develop a life of their own so that principles become confused with personalities. Arguments are, indeed, like a dripping-tap that needs to be mended.

I wonder how Jesus dealt with arguments? I'm quite glad that the disciples quarrelled over the best jobs in the Kingdom (*Mark* 9:33ff.) Firstly, Jesus confronts the situation boldly so that the argument doesn't smoulder and destroy the fellowship. It makes me realise that quarrels in churches are wrong, no matter what principles are involved. Believers may differ but they may *not* quarrel! Jesus says that his followers must quickly be reconciled and worship together in peace (*Matthew* 5:23f.) Whether I'm right or wrong is not the only issue to consider. As a follower of Jesus, I must find a way to make my point without dividing the fellowship.

Secondly, I see that Jesus quickly identifies the cause of the argument. "What were you arguing about?" he asks. Of course, he knows full well what the problem is but the disciples themselves must acknowledge it. They have to separate the issue itself from their own bruised *egos*. If ever I become obsessed with my own 'rightness', I'm tempted to exaggerate others' 'wrongness'. Very soon, I'm seeing myself as the noble Defender of Truth with a divine right to question the motives and morals of those who oppose me. That's the way quarrels grow!

Jesus' third step is to describe the atmosphere in which Christians must air their disagreements. "If you want the place of honour," Jesus tells his squabbling disciples, "you must serve others." Discussions must take place within a sphere of peaceable humility and love. Christians will have their differences but personal power-struggles have no place in churches. Jesus says that peacemakers are the 'children of God' who is the Supreme Peacemaker (*Matthew* 5:9). I must embrace my role as a 'closer of floodgates', a diffuser of quarrels, both my own and those of other people.

TODAY'S RESOLVE

Today, I will try to close floodgates.

"Lord, help me to watch my temper, especially if I foresee difficult situations on the horizon and make me a tactful peacemaker. Amen!"

25. REDEEMING GOSSIP

Proverbs 18:1-8

Key verse:-18:8 "There's nothing so delicious as the taste of gossip. It melts in your mouth."

I discover that it was the poet Catullus who wrote sarcastically about, "the rumours of crabbed, censorious old men". I hope that that's not a description of me but I'm afraid that there is part of me which finds it hard to resist rumour and gossip, even though as a Christian I ought to know better. Why, as the Wise Man says, do I find gossip "so delicious"?

Perhaps it's because rumours are tasty extras added to the main course of a conversation, "By the way, have you heard...?" Rumour has the appeal of forbidden fruit. It's very sound betrays it, coming as it does from 'a murmur' – doubtful information whispered surreptitiously in the ear. "Don't tell anybody else but I heard..." Above all else, rumour and gossip pander to my *ego.* I feel that I possess privileged information denied to the crowd.

I know that gossip and rumour are dangerous because, even if groundless, they can create their own reality and ruin lives. (I only have to think of the Nazis' rumours about the Jews which bore the terrifying fruit of the *holocaust*) I also know that breaking my addiction requires positive action. It isn't enough for me simply to say that I'll always tell the unvarnished truth because even truth *without* gossip needs careful handling.

Santayana may have exaggerated when he said that, "the truth is cruel" but knowing the truth doesn't necessarily make it right for me to blurt it out. Paul advises me to "speak the truth in love" (*Ephesians* 4:15). Sometimes, it seems more loving *not* to tell the whole truth. It's all rather confusing. Perhaps there's another way of dealing with my love of gossip.

Looking up our English word 'gossip' has given me an idea. Apparently, 'gossip' used to be a good word. Literally, it meant 'akin to God' which was why God-parents were known as 'gossips'. More generally, 'gossips' were special friends and so gossip became 'a friendly conversation'. That sounds a very positive approach. I can turn back the clock and redeem 'gossip' by restoring its original meaning. I can divert the energy I use for *bad* gossip into spreading *good* gossip. But that's not the end. I also discover that the word 'gossip' is connected with 'gospel'. It isn't just playing words. I can 'gossip the Gospel'. I can share my faith in 'friendly conversation' with those I meet.

TODAY'S RESOLVE

Today, I will redeem 'gossip'.

"Lord of Truth, save me from spreading or listening to unhelpful gossip and help me to find ways of gossiping the Gospel. Amen!"

DAY TWENTY-SIX

26. TIMID FAITH

Proverbs 18:10-19

Key verse:-18:15 "Everyone with good sense wants to learn."

Does one's mind become less plastic and pliable with age? Does it become less ready for new and disturbing ideas? There's certainly now part of me which wishes I could avoid intellectual hassle but, to be fair, I don't think that it is all just a matter of mental cowardice. It's partly due to the fact that I've come to realise that Christians who defend 'the old ways' have a point. Tradition is not necessarily bad and innovation is not necessarily good. Minds can be so 'open' that unworthy ideas fall through into acceptance without touching the sides! Perhaps I appreciate more than once I did that the Church has a responsibility to protect the historic faith against ephemeral fancies and I feel the need to play my part. But where do I draw the line? Often it is so hard for me to tell the difference between new insight and old heresy.

Perhaps I must begin by accepting the fact that I *do* have a proclivity to sustain the *status quo* and that this sits uncomfortably with the sort of adventurous faith which is always ready to reach out into the unknown. New knowledge is exploding around me in all directions and my theology must explode with it. I find advances in science fascinating and I need a commensurate, magnificent, Cosmic Gospel. It must be big enough to embrace the exciting new revelations of a

God whose true mystery science (usually reluctantly) is only just beginning to uncover. I admire Alice Meynell's vision of *Christ in the Universe* with its,

...million alien Gospels, in what guise

He trod the Pleiades, the Lyre, the Bear

I suppose that I myself am a sort of 'universe of possibilities' waiting to be explored and life is too short to tolerate boorish ignorance. When I stop learning, I stop living and, as the Wise Man reminds me, life requires a systematic search for new ideas about myself, my world and my God.

I accept that there is an element of risk in this. This is not a place for timid faith. It is not the spiritual stay-at-home but the faith-inspired explorer who risks getting lost. I still sadly remember a fine Christian friend whose search for new ideas led him into despairing atheism. I must retain a balance so that my proper respect for tradition accompanies continuous travel into the unknown. If my Lord is, indeed, 'the Way, the Truth and the Life', I can follow him, believing that he always has new truths to teach me.

TODAY'S RESOLVE

Today, I will actively seek new ideas.

"Lord Jesus, today teach me something me about yourself, myself and the world – even if it is something I would rather not know. Amen!"

27. PASSING THE BUCK

Proverbs 19:1-12

Key verse:-19:3 "We are ruined by our own stupidity though we blame the Lord."

I've just learned that 'passing the buck' is a poker-player's term for refusing to 'bid' (whatever that means!) However, it suits the Wise Man's allusions to people who ruin their lives and then blame God for their own stupid mistakes. They 'pass the buck' to God.

It is a child's earliest defence mechanism for dodging responsibility. A little girl's tee-shirt declared in large letters–*He did it!* Most of us still do it and, if all else fails; we blame God for not ordering things better. One of Tolstoy's leading characters in *War and Peace,* says, "O Lord, I have sinned but I have several excellent excuses", which sounds uncomfortably like some of my prayers!

Excuses are all about playing games with the truth, usually born of a childish craving for others' approval. They are a sign of immaturity, an inability to face life as it really is. By pretending that I'm better than I am, (and hopefully making others look worse than they are), I think that I can avoid taking responsibility for my own life and character.

I think again of the parable of the Great Feast in which God is the generous host whose friends all ingeniously excuse themselves from attending his dinner. (*Luke* 14:15-24) The host says, "Not one of the guests I first invited will get even a bite of my food!" God is not deceived even by my most ingenious excuses, so it's pointless for me to continue making them.

It also makes me think of the 'prodigal son' who "comes to himself", an old idiom which means 'seeing yourself without pretence'. (*Luke* 15:17) The boy suddenly becomes a man, no longer blaming others for his predicament. He stops pretending and decides to throw himself on his father's mercy. Refusing to make excuses is indeed a sign of maturity.

However, the father does not even listen to his son's carefully rehearsed apology; He is too busy hugging his long-lost son. Making excuses to God is not only unwise, it's unnecessary because he loves me just as I am. I simply need to come to him, acknowledging that I have been a silly idiot and blaming nobody but myself. As a Christian, I live by the motto which adorned the desk of President Harry S. Truman – *The Buck Stops Here!*

TODAY'S RESOLVE

Today, I will be very careful about making excuses.

"Lord, help me not to waste your time by making excuses and help me to judge others' excuses kindly, remembering that they're only doing what I also do. Amen!"

DAY TWENTY-EIGHT

28. "....A LENDER BE"

Proverbs 19:13-20

Key verse:-19:17 "Caring for the poor is lending to the Lord and you will be well repaid".

The Wise Man's picture makes me wince. It touches a sore place where my theology and practice diverge. My theology is more open-handed than my actions. Theologically, I know that everything comes from God and is his to use but, humanly, I want to control my time and money. The cautious part of me warms to Polonius' advice in *Hamlet,* "Neither a borrower nor a lender be."

The trouble is that God himself has set me such a glowing example of generosity. What annoys about his giving is that it seems so ill-advised. I like to help really the deserving, nice people but God displays a disconcerting enthusiasm for the undeserving. Jesus warned me about his Father's bizarre charitable policies (*Luke* 6:35) "God is good even to people who are unthankful." Worse still, God wants to squander <u>my</u> money, <u>my</u> time and <u>my</u> talents to carry out his rescue missions. It really is intolerable!

When I find myself thinking like that, I must try to remember that God's generosity is controlled by what is *needed* not by what is *deserved.* (Incidentally, I shudder to think what would happen to me if God gave *me* only what I deserve!). The Wise Man says that, when I let God use his gifts, "I will be well repaid" and Jesus often confirms that God heaps blessings on those who love and serve him.

Sometimes the reward for 'lending to God' is actually material. I remember the widow who, having emptied her cruse of oil for God's prophet, found that it was miraculously replenished. (*I Kings* 17:8ff.) Many Christians tell the same story. The more they 'lend' to God, the more he seems to replenish their resources. It's as though the laws of economics are overturned by greater, spiritual principles.

Normally, however, generosity to others leaves me materially poorer but God gives me rewards of a different kind. He gives me a sense of joy and harmony, attuned to his will. Jesus says that, when I lend, "without expecting to be paid back", I will 'get a great reward' and 'will be a true child of God.' (*Luke 6:35*) Each time I am obediently generous, I will understand a little more about my generous God who, so loved the world that he gave his only Son." (*John* 3:16)

TODAY'S RESOLVE

Today, I will actively look for a way to be extra generous.

"O generous God, today I will increase my donation to some worthy cause. As I do so, remind me to say, "Thank you, Father for giving your Son for me. Amen!"

29. THE GLORIOUS LIBERTY

Proverbs 19:20-29

Key verse:-19:21 "We may make a lot of plans but the Lord will do what he has decided"

This puzzles me. If God has already decided what's going to happen, what's the point of me planning *anything*? Were the Greeks right when they said that human freedom is only an illusion, a joke played on us by the gods? I can't believe that – but the question won't go away.

Perhaps I can tackle it this way. Jesus shows me that my life is controlled by a Heavenly Father who isn't a cheat and who doesn't play cynical games. God deals with me just like a wise human father who encourages his children to make their own plans so that they learn both from their successes and failures but who is always ready to step in to avert disaster.

God gives me free-will to develop my individuality and to be useful in his world. I notice that a more traditional version of this problem says, "There are many *plans* in a man's heart", using a word which can also mean 'to lay a fire'. What a splendid idea! God can use all my plans, both successes and failures, to fuel the greater fire of his grand design.

But I still have a problem. , Paul reminds me (*Romans* 7:15) that, even when I plan to 'do the right thing' I can be thwarted. I am not a completely free

67

agent. Quite apart from sin clouding my judgement, I can be caught in a web of circumstances beyond my control and find myself contributing to problems rather than solving them. My plans can do so much harm!

My hope is that the Wise Man is right when he says, that "the Lord will do what he has decided". It is a comfort to remember that, ultimately, all my plans (good, bad and indifferent) are provisional and that it is God who has the last word. My foolishness may hinder his purposes for a while but it can never totally defeat them. Perhaps this is what is meant by experiencing the 'glorious liberty of the children of God" (*Romans* 8:21). He opens my eyes to endless possibilities and gives me a chance to use the initiatives he has given me. I can be like a horse released to gallop in a limitless paddock or a fish freed to explore a boundless ocean. God gives me freedom to make my plans and then I can relax and allow him to take charge.

TODAY'S RESOLVE

Today, I will simply enjoy being a Christian.

"Heavenly Father, thank you for giving me options. Help me to plan wisely and then to relax and let you have your way. Amen!"

DAY THIRTY

30. GOD'S SEARCHLIGHT

Proverbs 20:23-30

Key verse:-20:27 "Our inner thoughts are a lamp from the Lord and they search our hearts".

Another translation of 'our inner thoughts' is 'our conscience' and the idea of conscience as God's searchlight' appeals to me. It reminds me of the times when, as a child in the Second World War, I peeped through the tiniest chink in the blackout curtains to watch the probing fingers of the searchlights trying to locate enemy aircraft. I like the idea that God has placed a searchlight-battery in my life to locate marauding temptations before they can destroy me.

I was brought up to believe Jiminy Cricket's advice to Pinocchio, "always let your conscience be your guide" but, in practice, I have found that it's not so simple. It's not just that I often ignore the clear guidance of my conscience but that I sense there's something suspicious about my conscience itself. I wonder what *conscience* really is. Who is 'inner me' who stands back and judges my action and motives? Whatever it is, it doesn't always seem to work as it ought. It both excuses things that are wrong and agonizes over things that are right.

I know that the Bible is cautious about the idea of *conscience*. Paul says that, following my conscience isn't good enough because my conscience itself can be

69

"weak and defiled" (*I Corinthians* 8:17) –literally, *sick* and *stained.* The trouble is that human consciences are so malleable. They can be crippled by ignorance, hardened by cruelty and dulled by indulgence. Society's cry goes up, "It's only human" and individual conscience capitulates. Once dubbed a 'natural habit' almost any vice becomes acceptable. This is a particular problem in our society which stresses personal preference and makes individual conviction the Supreme Court against which there is no appeal.

At least I can try to put my own house in order. My conscience may be what George Washington called, "a little spark of celestial fire" but it glows uncertainly and needs some attention. One of the promises I find in my Bible is that God's offers to give me, "a clear conscience" (*I Timothy* 1:19) and I want to take up his invitation. I want God to clear every nook and cranny of my darkened and confused conscience so that it can become his searchlight, illuminating my intentions, being sound in judgement and irresistible in its effect.

TODAY'S RESOLVE

Today, I will remember that human consciences can make mistakes (including mine!)

"Lord of light, shine into my judgements and decisions today. Show me what is right and then give me strength to do it. Amen!"

31. RULES AND REGULATIONS

Proverbs 12:1-8

Key verse:-12:6 Teach your children right from wrong and when they are grown they will still do right.

It's hard to be good parents these days. So many of the sign-posts for living that I knew as a child have been removed. The Wise Man may be too optimistic when he says that well-trained children never stray in later life but nobody doubts the effect of early influences. I am so grateful that my own parents enabled me to assimilate Christian values by a process of loving spiritual osmosis but the proverb raises the issue of discipline in my life.

I heard a distinguished educationalist say, "Many children are crippled today by their parents' inability to say 'No'." Adults and children alike need guidance to delineate the boundaries of acceptable behaviour. Some contemporary theologies seems to regard rules as 'unchristian' and posit a *laissez faire* God who excuses almost anything but Jesus gives clear, non-negotiable commandments and sets down an unequivocal Rule of Life.

Jesus taught the importance and dangers of rules because he knew that our spiritual growth requires a discipline greater than ourselves. There is a Discipline of Grace which refuses to be controlled by my passing whims and frivols of convenience or to evaporate before the claims of laziness. Such rules give structure to my everyday Christian living. Without them, I become spiritually flabby. Most of my sins are sins of stupidity, impulsive rather than cynical and premeditated. Against such maverick temptations, the warning bells of discipline can be very effective.

Another thought – disciplined obedience is also a powerful testimony. At the appointed hour, the young Moslem who tried to teach me Kiswahili, would courteously entrust us to his assistant and withdraw to pray. Such rules not only punctuated his day, they challenged my own vacillating Christian devotional life. They made me ask, "When did *I* last testify by making it clear that the disciplines of my faith have absolute priority in my life?" The experience made me realise that I am far too willing to subordinate my devotional disciplines to the convenience of myself and others. Perhaps the time has come for me to review the rules which undergird my daily walk with God.

TODAY'S RESOLVE

Today, I will take an honest look at the state of my spiritual discipline.

"Lord of loving discipline, show me where my devotional life has become disorganized and my code of conduct too accommodating. Help me to take the necessary steps to put both right. Amen!"

32. LORD, I'M TIRED!

Proverbs 22:4-16

Key verse:-22:13 "Don't be so lazy that you say, if I go to work, a lion will eat me!"

This is a sort of verbal cartoon, a caricature of an idler whose ridiculous excuse for staying in bed is that, if he goes to work, he might be eaten by a lion. Beneath the joke there lies the truth that idleness is an attitude of mind, a loss of motivation to act. There is a kind of spiritual idleness which can descend upon the soul. I've known sincere Christians who, one minute are full of faith and good works, and, the next, have been rendered spiritually catatonic by a strange and frustrating spiritual emptiness.

It makes me remember that the Mediaeval spiritual experts identified this condition and gave it a name –*accidie.* According the great Methodist Samuel Chadwick (*The Sin of Accidie*) it is what happens to Christians when, "listlessness, apathy, dejection, depression, gloominess and inertia" all meet in their soul. It seems that even the greatest Christians have had this experience so we must all be vulnerable. It can happen to me!

I strongly suspect that one of the commonest causes of *accidie* is spiritual 'burn-out' and exhaustion. The overburdened soul simply 'shuts up shop' and, like the idler in the proverb, it makes all kinds of excuses for staying in bed. Sincere believers can become so exhausted by excessive 'church work', that keeping the ship of faith afloat eventually demands just too much effort and it sinks.

Looking back, I realise that sometimes I have experienced touches of *accidie*, albeit rarely and in a non-terminal form. I don't think that I've diagnosed it correctly at the time, putting it down to overwork and frustration with the faults of the Church. Providentially, I've managed to come through it by clinging to the simple idea that, just as the moon still exists even when it is hidden by clouds, so God remains Unchanging Love even when I don't feel it. Believing this, I've then had enough sense to tell him honestly, "Lord, I'm tired of it all!" and, like David, I have "poured out my complaint". (*Psalms* 142:2) After a while, God has restored my sense of realism, reminding me that I'm not Superman. He has sorted out my priorities by showing me how to re-shuffle life's cards and to discard the unnecessary ones. If *accidie* returns, I may need to remember all this afresh

TODAY'S RESOLVE

Today, I will watch for signs of *accidie*.

"Encouraging Lord, even if I am spared *accidie* today, I may meet hardworking Christians who are in its grip, help me to recognize this and to encourage them. Amen!"

DAY THIRTY-THREE

33. CHRISTIAN CONSERVATISM

Proverbs 22:17-29

Key verse:-22:28 "Don't move a boundary marker set up by your ancestors."

Having lived among subsistence farmers, I understand the outrage expressed in this proverb. They believe that God owns all land and trustingly lends it to each succeeding generation. Therefore, tampering with ancient boundaries defrauds the living, insults the dead and challenges God himself. It has made me think about our own society's careless violation of sacred traditions.

Some old ways must go. This age demands nimble minds that grasp new concepts and use new technologies. However, life today seems to be breathless. Nothing abides. 'Old' and 'useless' so often are synonyms and yet, at the same time, we are torn between idolizing the new and pining for the old. We're obsessed by the latest technology but we're also crazy about family-trees, ancient buildings, history and antiques. It is as though, in the midst of constant change, we cannot bear the thought of being rootless. Deep down, we sense that shifting ancient boundary-stones too easily is theft and a cavalier uprooting of landmarks cheats generations to come. We need our past to explain our present and inspire our future.

Nevertheless, the fact remains that the annual death-toll of traditions is very high and it has certainly ravaged European Christianity where Christian rituals are often just quaint folk-memories, dusted off for civic occasions or displayed to boost the tourist industry. Having lost the religious tools for dealing with life's crises, parents have also denied them to their children and their children's children.

I was once an iconoclastic smasher of traditions. Now I'm not so sure. I know that Christians must be contemporary but there's a real need for a Ministry of Conservation. Mine is a historical faith, rooted in certain treasured beliefs and practices and I need to hear the prophet's words, "Look to the rock whence you were hewn and the pit whence you were digged" (*Isaiah* 51:1- I still cherish its AV version.) The words toll like a warning bell! While avoiding a Luddite resistance to all change, I must defend sound, Christian conservatism. By refusing to move the boundary-stones at least, I am a stubborn reminder of eternal verities in a frenetic society which is frightened by its own celerity.

TODAY'S RESOLVE

Today, I will be proud of the faith-traditions I have inherited.

"Unchanging God, I thank you for the traditions which hold me steady in a changing world. Help me to distinguish between lasting verities and outdated custom. Amen!"

DAY THIRTY-FOUR

34. SHUTTING MY EYES

Proverbs 24:1-12

Key verse:-24:12 "Don't say, 'I didn't know it!' God can read your mind....and knows your thoughts."

Pretending that "I didn't know" has been popular ever since Adam pleaded innocence with an apple-core in his hand It's my self-preservation 'damage limitation' mechanism which reinterprets uncomfortable information. It is one of the most serpentine of all temptations because its subtle self-deception seems to justify bare-faced lies.

For instance, I don't think that the priest and the Levite were especially evil men when they left that victim on the Jericho road. They just convinced themselves that somebody better qualified would soon come to his aid. (*Luke* 10:31f.) They simply did not want to believe the evidence of their eyes. Fortunately, the Samaritan saved the day. Pretended ignorance is diabolical device. "The only thing necessary for the triumph of evil is for good men to do nothing" said Edmund Burke and how often history has proved him right - atrocities perpetrated because good people pleaded counterfeit ignorance and millions starving because well-fed people say, "We didn't know"!

But can pretended ignorance ever actually be a virtue? I think of Peter in the High Priest's house denying that he knows Jesus (*Matthew* 26:70ff.) Why

77

does he do it when he knows that he's lying? Peter may have had many faults but he wasn't a coward. Was he trying to buy time to formulate a rescue plan? Was his pretended ignorance a sin or a brave and loving gesture?

I think that I really do try to tell the truth no matter how inconvenient it may be but, like Peter, I still find the subtler variations of pretended ignorance much trickier. How do I know when my pretending not to know is due to personal cowardice and when it is honest consideration for another's need? I like the old version of this proverb which says that "God weighs the heart" and I find that very comforting. He knows my motives as well as my actions and, if I have the sense to hold my tongue for a little while longer, he will show me what to say and when to say it.

TODAY'S RESOLVE

Today, I will pay special attention to my personal integrity.

"Lord Jesus, you are Truth. Save me from 'bending the truth' to extricate myself from awkward situations but also show me when it is right to withhold sensitive information. Amen!"

35. DANGEROUS LIASONS

Proverbs 25:21-28

Key verse:-25:26 "When a good person gives in to the wicked, it's like dumping garbage in a stream of clear water."

I like the translation 'compromise with 'instead of 'give in'. 'Compromise' ('a common promise') is such a seductive, comfortable word but the Wise Man tells me that it has its shadow-side. To compromise with evil people is to make an unholy alliance. But it's not quite as simple as that.

How do I know exactly *when* I should compromise? Being a Christian seems to give me special problems where compromise is concerned. I'm supposed to be so 'Christianly' tolerant, loving everybody, forgiving their failings and absorbing the wrongs they inflict. So, how do I know when 'enough is enough'? When does tolerance become unacceptable compromise? God's decision to let the weeds and wheat grow together hasn't exactly helped because it seems like a sort of compromise. (*Matthew* 13:25ff.) If only he would neatly label and remove all the evil people, I wouldn't have to make so many difficult judgements.

Getting it right is important because compromising with evil people is "like dumping garbage into a stream of clear water". I remember, when living in the Panamanian jungle, I watched

Guaymi Indian women washing their clothes. They always washed where the river entered the sea to ensure that the upper reaches of the river remained unpolluted for drinking-water. Similarly, one single act of unwise compromise with evil on my part could pollute the lives of those around me.

Compromise still remains seductive. It sounds so sensible when it requires only the slightest deviation from perfect integrity. It is so in tune with the permissive, 'live and let live' mood of the age and, often, right and wrong diverge so imperceptibly that it takes a long time to reveal the disastrous effects of compromising between them.

But being a Christian doesn't mean that I have to please everybody. In the desert, Jesus was *very un*compromising! He sent the devil packing with his offer of 'sensible', compromising short-cuts to success. (*Matthew* 4:1-11) I'll arm myself with Christ's proof-texts as alarms to sound when compromise is dangerous. They will give me time to think. It's much better for me to say, "I need time to think" than risk 'dangerous liaisons' that I may later regret,

TODAY'S RESOLVE

Today, I will be on my guard against deceptive compromises.

"Lord, you know what it is to be tempted to compromise. If I am tempted to compromise unwisely today, help me to know, however subtle it may be so that I can resist it. Amen! "

36. FUELLING FELLOWSHIP

Proverbs 26:17-28

Key verse:-26:20 "Where there is no fuel a fire goes out; where there is no gossip arguments come to an end."

I don't want to return to the theme of *gossip* because it's not just gossip that dies if 'unfuelled'; it is true of *all* human interaction. Relationships have to be worked at or, like a fire; they will die for lack of fuel. I have reason to want to apply this especially to the Church

I can be very scathing about the Church which stubbornly refuses to do things *my* way but what blessings I have received through Christian relationships! For all its faults, I thank God for the Church. It is a miracle of divine social engineering. The first Christians found their new relationship so wonderful that they coined a word to describe it. They baptized the original meaning of our word 'fellowship' Christian fellowship is the product of faith in Christ and is fuelled by mutual respect and loving concern. (e.g. *I Corinthians* 1:9, *Philippians* 1:5). Churches are intended to be showcases of wonderful relationships, shop-windows against which a fragmented world may press its nose to see people living in harmony.

I have often fiercely declared that "churches are not social clubs" but there is a lovely sense in which they do fit the dictionary definition. They truly are, "associations of persons united by common interest, meeting periodically for cooperation". John Wesley's opponents paid him an unwitting compliment when they nicknamed his Oxford followers 'The Holy Club'. I am continually amazed by the way in which a common love for Christ is a *centripetal f*orce drawing together peoples of varied in age and interests. Yes, there is a wonderful sense in which churches I know are 'holy clubs'!

However, there are also *centrifugal* forces at work in congregations, separating us and throwing us away from one another. Pride, stubbornness, greed and vanity all play their part and, unless we constantly refuel the fire by seeing Christ in each other, the fellowship smoulders and dies. What challenges me is that it only takes one person to set those conflicting forces in motion. One thoughtless word can ignite a process of destruction in a congregations but, equally, one loving person can reconcile a separated fellowship. I hope that I may never be the former and always be the latter but it will require my constant vigilance.

TODAY'S RESOLVE

Today, I will fuel my relationships with love.

"Lord, today I will see the best in the people I meet (especially those I find it hard to like) remembering how much you have to tolerate in me! Please help me. Amen!"

DAY THIRTY-SEVEN

37. SENSITIVITY

Proverbs 27:8-14

Key verse:-27: 14 "A loud greeting in the morning is the same as a curse"

I love this proverb. As an inveterate early riser, I'm scolded for being too lively too early and for being insensitive to people who need to slide into their day later and more gradually. However, this verse leads me to consider a much greater principle. I must not assume that mine is the only right approach to life and I must learn to be more sensitive to other people's preferences.

The ancient Greeks apparently had a word for the sensitivity I need. They used to talk about *empatheia*, which means 'getting inside' a situation in order to understand it properly. I think of Jesus "knowing what people were really like" (*John* 2:25), entering other people's minds. Judas, Mary, Martha, Matthew, Zacchaeus - all were open books to Jesus. It's just a little of that genius that I covet for myself.

I notice that Jesus never avoided anybody simply because he did not like what he saw. Outward appearances can be deceptive. We all continually send out soundless signals and it is so easy to misread them. I urgently need to learn how to meet people without pre-judging them. I'm far too easily influenced by the way others appear. I look frequently before I listen but how I resent it when people do the same to me!

There's something else that strikes me. Jesus accepted that people are different from each other. He didn't expect Mary to be Martha or Peter to be John. He never forced people to change but simply showed them their hidden possibilities and then left the rest to them. Why is it, then, that I can't stop meddling in other people's lives and trying to change them? I must learn to accept and love people as they are even when I don't like what I see.

However, there is a trap. Trumpeting my own open-mindedness and sensitivity towards other people can become simply a hypocritical device for trying to court popularity. I must never confuse *accepting* other people's differences with *approving* of them. I must not be so eager to accommodate others' views that I compromise my own principles. However, when I do have to differ from other people, I pray for sensitivity to make my testimony both effective and winsome.

TODAY'S RESOLVE

Today, I will stop before making snap-judgements about the people I meet.

"Lord, you love us all just as we are; help me to see the best in everybody I meet today. Amen!"

38. 'FOLDING MY LEGS' WITH GOD

Proverbs 27:17-27

Key verse:-27:17 "Just as iron sharpens iron, friends sharpen the minds of each other."

Conversation is such a precious gift. When people talk, their ideas strike sparks off each other. I once lived among people who loved to sit outside their houses in the cool of the tropical evening and talk late into the night.

Conversation seems to be addictive. I still find it odd that the same people who seem normally to communicate largely in monosyllabic grunts will converse enthusiastically by 'texts' and mobile 'phones. In chat rooms, they will share their most intimate secrets with cyber friends whom they never meet in the flesh. Perhaps that is the appeal. Like so much post-modern living, cyber-conversations are ephemeral, ended at any time without the participants having to reveal their true identity.

All this has made me ponder the true nature of *conversation*. I've found that, originally, it meant 'to keep company with' and it reminded me of my parents' quaint use of that expression. A couple who were 'keeping company' were in love and would eventually marry. Is that the secret of true conversation? It requires commitment, a readiness to give time and effort to the exercise. I recall that Samuel Johnson complained to Boswell that talking to John Wesley was like trying to hit a moving target. I've looked up the quotation. "He is always obliged to go at a certain hour," complained the exasperated Doctor, which "is very disagreeable to a man who loves to fold his legs and have out his talk, as I do." In these days when I, like many others, am swept along on waves of schedules, I need to remember afresh that they are no substitute for taking time to talk to one another with real commitment.

Reading between the lines of the Gospels, I think that Jesus must have spent many hours just talking to his disciples and even more talking to his Father. Conversing with God – now that's a fruitful idea! I confess that my prayers are often much more like brief monologues than healthy conversations. I'm so busy telling God how to organize his world that he can't get a word in edgeways! That is not a proper conversation. Conversation means speaking *and* listening. I need times when I 'fold my legs and have my talk out' with God, without rushing away to keep some appointment or to satisfy some unimportant whim. Only then will the Divine Mind begin to strike sparks of mine and reveal new truths.

TODAY'S RESOLVE

Today, I will make time for a genuine conversation with God.

"Lord, instead of clock-watching in my Quiet Time, I will relax, stop talking and listen to you. Amen!"

39. IGNORANCE AND BLISS

Proverbs 29:12-22

Key verse:-29:18 "Without guidance from God law and order disappear but God blesses everyone who obeys the Law".

Is the world really more wicked than it was or is it just that the devil has improved his media skills and we hear more about him? No! I'm not just a 'godly grouser'. I believe that, wherever I look, I see this proverb confirmed.

Abroad I see the organized and brutal elimination of Christianity and, in this country, I see it fighting for breath beneath a scum of aggressive secularism as 'evangelistic' humanists effectively convince people that atheism is now the norm. Even where some belief remains, people are encouraged to indulge their own personal do-it-yourself faiths and bizarre spiritualities.

Many people believe in God in the same way that they believe in China or the Eiffel Tower. God is an object to be visited when the fancy takes. 'God' can be anything from Bambi to Attila the Hun but it doesn't really matter since God's only needed for the occasional emergency. There's just enough faith to inoculate against the real thing, producing technical believers but practical atheists 'without guidance from God'.

Having pensioned off its God, in many ways, society 'sees law and order disappear'. Moral self-policing can so easily produce ethical chaos. In the name of personal freedom, marriage becomes 'repression' and pornography 'liberty'. The poet was right, "ignorance is bliss" when "'tis folly to be wise". (Thomas Grey, *On a Distant Prospect of Eton College).*

But I still have a problem. Truth is so untidy. 'Religion' does not equal 'goodness' nor does 'atheism' equal 'badness'. People without God can be good when they ought to be miserable failures! Job complained about the prosperity of 'the godless wicked' (e.g. *Job* 24) but my complaint is about the 'godless *good*'! I know that, the Holy Spirit is working in all goodness but I wish that people would recognize God at work in their lives *incognito*.

Often, I feel helpless to change things but I can, at least, show how good it is to "obey God's laws". Paul says, "*be constrained* by the love of Christ" (*II Corinthians* 5:14) – a word also used of besieging a city. What a wonderful idea! I am *besieged* by the love of Christ. There is a barrier between me and the confusion of society and I may live safely with him even in a crazy world.

TODAY'S RESOLVE

Today, I will try to show the joy of living by Christian standards.

"Lord, if today I have to stand against the crowd on a matter of principle, help me to do so tactfully and winsomely. Amen!"

40. THE HIDE AND SEEK GOD

Proverbs 30:1-10

Key verse:-30:2f "I'm far too stupid to be considered human. I never was wise and I don't understand what God is like"

I've been thinking about 'the right to know' – that 'sacred cow' of contemporary society. It spawns the belief that we may intrude on others' privacy, boosts the circulation of the tabloids and lines the pockets of scurrilous biographers. We judge people by selective snippets, innuendos and misquotations, admiring or damning them on the basis of trivia.

I'm not completely guiltless. Sometimes, I've judged people on insufficient evidence only to realise that I haven't really known them at all. My 'saints' have committed uncharacteristic sins and my 'sinners' have displayed unprecedented virtues. No wonder the bemused Wise Man sighs "I cannot understand humans" (I think it's a better translation of verse 2)

I probably understand myself least of all. The Delphic Oracle's "Know thyself!" isn't simple. Like Paul, I often feel, "I don't understand why I act the way I do. I don't do what I know is right. I do the things I hate. (*Romans* 7:15) The proverb is right. If I can't understand human beings, how can I ever hope to understand God? Lines from Pope's school-learned poem suddenly sound like very good advice: "Know, then, thyself, presume not God to scan, The proper study of mankind is man." (*Essay on Man*)

However, I just can't stop 'scanning' God'! God is such a tantalizing mystery. God affronts my 'right to know'. God decrees without my approval, moves without explanation, disappears and reappears without farewells or apologies. God seems to ignore my prayers without excuse and pursues plans regardless of my protests. How can I hope to understand such a maverick, hide-and-seek God?

The truth is that I *cannot* understand God. I have no 'right to know'. God is God and I am not! The devil's syllogism is, "I cannot understand God, therefore God does not exist"– a piece of incredibly stupid reasoning, a *non sequitur* of gargantuan proportions. It is my perception, not God's perfection that is at fault. I believe that God exists and that Jesus shows me as much of God as I can cope with. For the rest, I surrender my 'right to know'. Faith' means allowing my 'right to know' to be swallowed up in absolute trust in a God whose intentions I need never fear even when they are a complete mystery.

TODAY'S RESOLVE

Today, I will look for signs of God and be content.

"Lord of mystery, beyond anything my little mind can understand, make me content to know you through Jesus. Amen!"

P.S. ISN'T IT A PITY?

+ ONE DAY

Isn't it a pity that there are only forty days in Lent?

If there had been forty-one, there might have been time to look at the very end of the book with its remarkable poem, 'In Praise of a Good Wife'.

The song may not satisfy all the criteria of modern feminism but it is still worth reading, especially the last verse of entire book –

"Show her respect- praise her in public for what she has done."

I find it strangely moving that the last words from the Wise Men should be a call to respect women. They really were wise!

So my journey with the Wise Men has ended. Thank you for looking over my shoulder.

I hope that eavesdropping on a 'jobbing Christian' has set off much more wonderful Lenten thoughts in your own mind.

Thank you for sticking with me. I'll miss you.

Lightning Source UK Ltd.
Milton Keynes UK
UKOW04f2118130116

266358UK00001B/1/P